John Knowles'

A Separate Peace

BookCaps™ Study Guide
www.bookcaps.com

Table of Contents

Historical Context

John Knowles was born in West Virginia in 1926. In 1941, at the age of fifteen, Knowles left home to attend Phillips Exeter Academy, a boarding school in New Hampshire, from which he graduated in 1945.

Upon graduation, he spent less than one year in the Air Force and subsequently attended Yale University, from which he graduated in 1949. Upon graduation from Yale, Knowles was employed as a freelance writer as well as a journalist.

It was Knowles' friend and fellow Yale alumnus Thornton Wilder who convinced him to continue his pursuits as a writer, and he was successful in publishing numerous short stories before having his first novel, "A Separate Peace", published in 1959. Though Knowles had eight other novels published, none of them had the success of his first. "A Separate Peace" has been critically acclaimed and continues to be very successful to this day.

As the adage goes, "write what you know", and that is exactly what Knowles did. "A Separate Peace" is set in a boarding school, much like the one Knowles attended in his adolescence.

The character of Gene Forrester is a lot like Knowles in that he is a transplant from the South, attending a boarding school in the New England area during the Second World

War. Many of the activities and characters in the novel are based on experiences that Knowles himself witnessed and was party to at Exeter. Knowles has made it clear that the more vicious and darker themes of the novel are purely fictional, as he greatly enjoyed his time at Exeter and did not have the same negative experiences as his characters.

Plot

Gene Forrester is a sixteen year old boy attending summer classes at Devon School, a private boarding school in New Hampshire. Gene is good friends with Phineas ("Finny"), his roommate, and another boy named Elwin Lepellier ("Leper"). It becomes obvious that all is not sunshine and roses between Gene and Finny as Gene is jealous of Finny's charm and knack for getting away with everything, as well as his superior athletic skills.

An accident happens one day when the boys are going to jump out of a tree, and Finny falls and shatters his leg, which is the end of his athletic career. Gene feels bad; worrying it is his fault that Finny fell because he made the branch shake, though Finny believes it to be an accident. When the boys come back to school for the Fall Finny it still at home recovering and Gene visits him to confess that it is his fault Finny fell.

Finny is furious with Gene but does not want to believe that it is true. Back at school one of the senior boys makes a joke that Gene pushed Finny on purpose, so he could have their room to himself, and tensions run high.

The boys all become preoccupied with the fact there is a war going on and they would all like to fight in it, rather than stay in school (WWII). When Finny returns to school he and Gene patch things up, putting Gene's confession behind them. Finny begins training Gene to be an athlete in his place and to hopefully become an Olympian.

Leper decides to join the Army, but soon goes AWOL which he announces in a letter to Gene. Back at school the other boys relentlessly accuse Gene of pushing Finny out of the tree, and Leper takes their side, believing that Gene did, in fact, cause the fall. Finny hobbles off on his crutches in total distress and falls down the hard marble steps of the school, breaking his leg all again.

Gene visits Finny before his operation, and they make peace, which is good because Finny does not live through the operation. The novel concludes with Knowles' views on peace and war and the notion of enemies.

Characters

Gene Forrester

The narrator of the novel and a student at Devon who grew up in the south. When the novel opens, Gene is visiting the school as an adult and reflecting on the time he spent there, starting with the summer session in which his life changed forever.

Throughout the novel, Gene is tormented with the idea that he caused his best friend and roommate, Finny, to fall from a tree, breaking his leg, out of jealousy and resentment. Gene is a good student and obeys the rules, except when Finny convinces him to break them. He and Finny have a very tight bond that almost seems toxic, though they rely on one another more than even they seem to know.

Phineas (Finny)

Finny is a tremendous athlete who has broken many school records, extremely charming, a bit of a rebel, and well-liked by everyone. Despite that the fact that Finny is athletic he is not competitive as he would rather have a good time playing a sport than win, which is why the games he invents do not usually have teams.

Gene admires and is jealous of Finny's relaxed attitude on life and his carefree outlook and even sees him as a sort of super-human, even though Finny is a poor student which is what matters to Gene the most. Finny falls from a tree, shattering his leg and taking sports away from him forever and eventually re-breaks it which leads to his death.

Elwin Lepellier (Leper)

Leper is a bit of a dreamer and lives in his own head in a world where there is nothing wrong, much like Finny who refuses to believe there is a war going on. Leper loves nature and being outdoors, choosing to cross-country ski to find a beaver dam rather than help the other boys shovel off the train tracks for the troops that will be passing through.

Leper believes that Gene shook the tree branch on purpose so that Finny would fall, which scares Gene. Leper joins the army when he finds out that he can ski there, though he soon goes a bit crazy and goes AWOL before they can give him a section eight discharge.

Brinker Hadley

Brinker is a tough senior boy who is a model student as he gets good grades and participates in many of the school organizations. He moves into the room that Leper had previously lived in when the winter session starts as Leper had been moved to a different dorm.

Brinker has a knack for writing bad poetry and a thirst to enlist in the military, which he and Gene decide to do until Finny comes back to school and Gene decides he no longer wants to leave. Brinker makes it his mission to prove that Gene pushed Finny out of the tree, and his persistence in the matter eventually leads to Finny's death. Brinker decided against the war at one point, and upon, graduation joined the Coast Guard, so he would not be drafted, much to the disappointment of his war-loving father.

Chet Douglass

Chet is also a student at Devon and is one of the boys who is at the tree the day Finny and Gene jump for the first time. Chet is usually in the group of boys that Gene and Finny find themselves surrounded with as he participates in Finny's attempts to alleviate the boredom of Devon – blitzball and the carnival.

Chet is a great student, like Gene, and is the biggest competition for Gene in terms of becoming valedictorian. The difference between Gene and Chet is that Gene is very competitive and needs to prove that he is the best at something but Chet just genuinely likes to learn and study.

Dr. Stanpole

Dr. Stanpole is the doctor on campus at Devon and runs the infirmary. The Doctor is the one who looks after Finny in both instances where his leg is broken, and communicates with Gene mostly about Finny's condition, knowing they are close.

It is Dr. Stanpole who has to tell Gene that Finny died while having his leg reset after the second break, and he is very regretful about it, knowing that, with the war going on, the boys are going to lose a lot of their friends. He says that a piece of marrow must have dislodged and travelled to Finny's heart, killing him.

Mr. Patch-Withers

Mr. Patch-Withers is the substitute headmaster of Devon while the school is in summer session. He is very strict and seems basically emotionless. Mr. Patch-Withers and his wife have some of the boys over for tea one afternoon, which seems an awkward experience for all involved except for Finny who is the center of attention and very animated.

At first he is upset that Finny has worn a pink shirt and used his school tie as a belt but when Finny explains himself in his charming way Mr. Patch-Withers clearly admires him and actually laughs.

Mr. Ludsbury

Mr. Ludsbury is the regular headmaster at Devon School. When the boys return for the fall semester, he has a talk with Gene about his disregard for the rules during summer session and is surprised with his lack of discipline as Gene is generally a quite disciplined student. When Gene and Finny tells the headmaster about the Olympic training that Gene is doing Mr. Ludsbury reminds them that any training done on campus will be for the war, to which Finny replies "no", shocking Mr. Ludsbury as he is not accustomed to being talk-backed to.

Quackenbush

Quackenbush is the captain of the crew team who ridicules Gene relentlessly when he wishes to become manager of the team. Managers are generally disabled students, not perfectly healthy and athletic ones, though Gene knows the reason he does not want to play any sports is because Finny can no longer play sports. Quackenbush calls Gene by his last name, "Forrester", and his relentless teasing of Gene leads to them getting in a scuffle and falling in the very dirty river where the crew team practices. Like many of the boys, Quackenbush wishes to join the military upon graduating.

Hazel Brewster

Though Hazel never appears in the story, as Devon is an all-boys school, she is somewhat of a legend and is presumably a very pretty girl from town. During the carnival, there is a snow sculpture made of her likeness, and also a lock of her hair, somehow obtained, is set to be one of the carnival prizes.

Brownie Perkins

Brownie is Brinker Hadley's roommate and is a bit of a servant for Brinker, all too gladly. Brownie has the very important job of guarding the hard cider while the boys are preparing for the winter carnival and he is also the boy who delivers Gene a telegram from Leper. Leper's telegram reveals to Gene that he has escaped and will be at the "Christmas location." Brownie is a very timid boy, and it is obvious that he just wants to fit in with the other boys and be accepted as one of the group.

Mr. Carhart

Mr. Carhart is the chaplain of the school and leads the church ceremony each morning. Mr. Carhart believes that God is aiding the Americans in fighting the war, though Finny adamantly believes that the war is made up by fat old men who sit around and want to control the youth.

After Leper goes AWOL from the army and sneaks back onto campus, Mr. Carhart is who he visits first, as he is obviously in a bad mental state and in need of some guidance.

Phil Latham

Phil Latham is the wrestling coach at Devon School. He is one of the men the boys seek for help after Finny falls down the marble stairs as he is trained in first aid. He helps Finny to relax and helps Dr. Stanpole to get Finny to the infirmary safely. While Finny is in the infirmary, Phil Latham gives Gene some wrestling tips to, unsuccessfully, keep his mind off things.

Mrs. Lepellier

Mrs. Lepellier is Leper's mother. Gene meets Mrs. Lepellier when he goes to Vermont to meet Leper upon receiving his telegram. Gene assumes that Leper has escaped from spies as it would be silly of him to escape from the army. However, Gene finds that Leper has gone AWOL and is having some serious mental issues which causes him to lash out, out of fear, which concerns Mrs. Lepellier greatly. She is mad at Gene for attacking her son who she says is "ill" but she eventually forgives him when he agrees to stay for lunch and is very polite and thankful to her.

Mr. Hadley

Mr. Hadley is Brinker's father, and Gene meets him at the end of the school year. Mr. Hadley seems to be one of the fat old men who love war that Finny was always talking about. He shares his thoughts on war with Brinker and Gene, neither of whom appreciate his stand though Gene seems to understand where he is coming from, much to Brinker's dismay. He believes that Gene and Brinker are weak for being pacifists and states that he enjoyed fighting in the First World War. Brinker thinks that his father and others who fought in WWI are the reason that WWII is happening.

Themes

Envy

While Gene and Finny are friends, it is obvious that Gene is envious of Finny. Gene is envious of Finny's athletic ability, his nonchalance, his charm, and his ability to keep himself out of trouble in any situation. Gene is quite uptight, very competitive, and wrongly mistakes Finny for being competitive as well, not ever realizing that Finny actually admires his smarts.

It is Gene's envy of Finny that fuels their entire friendship that is often toxic though Finny does not mean for it to be. Envy is what causes Gene to subconsciously make the tree branch shake causing Finny's fall.

Identity

When Gene was first moving from the south to go to Devon he thought he may have to act like someone else to fit in, but he soon realized that he could just be himself. Gene has a hard time dealing with the person he is and often wishes that he could be like others, specifically Finny.

Gene does not realize that others are impressed by the person he is and his intelligence, especially Finny, and he wastes his time competing with them and being jealous. Even Brinker believes that he wants to enlist but then realizes that he does not agree with the war nor does he want any part of it. It is often difficult to come to grips with one's identity during adolescence, and it is no different for the boys at Devon.

Friendship

Though the relationship between Gene and Finny may seem toxic, due to Gene's preoccupation with competition and jealousy, the boys really do rely on each other and their friendship quite a bit. Gene actually feels as though he and Finny are so close that they are two parts of a whole and need one another to survive.

Everything Finny and Gene do is together, and, while it seems at first like Gene needs Finny around, it is really Finny who needs Gene to keep his mind off the harsh realities of the war. The two boys have not just a friendship with an overwhelming reliance on one another.

Youth

The boys at Devon are living in a haven that is guarded by their youth. Devon is the place where the boys can be separated from what is going on in the world and with the war. As long as the boys are still in their youth they are safe from being drafted and thus can enjoy their last year or so as an adolescent before being forced to grow up in the face of warfare. Ironically Finny, who never wanted to be faced with war but finally admitted that it was really happening, did not live to be old enough to be drafted to the war he tried so hard to deny.

Rebellion

Most of the rebellion at Devon School is at the hands of Finny who gets away with it due to his ability to charm the pants off anyone he comes into contact with. Finny fully embraces his youth and refuses to grow up to face the realities of the world and takes advantage of finding the fun in everything he does and going through life with a very relaxed and carefree attitude.

When the realities of the war begin to face the boys at Devon some of them, such as Brinker, decide that they want nothing to do with it and rebel against society's expectations. In most cases, the rebellion seems a catalyst for refusing to take life seriously.

Memory

The concept of memory in this novel is not very reliable as the characters often second guess themselves and never seem to know exactly what happened and when. Gene seems to remember everything about Devon when he visits the school as an adult, but no one can seem to remember exactly what happened the day Finny fell from the tree as the stories are always changing.

Gene feels like maybe he made Finny fall on purpose, but is not sure though he feels very guilty about it. Leper feels sure he saw Gene make Finny fall but later is not sure either. Finny does not really remember anything and changes his idea of what happened several times. It seems that memory is all speculation and no facts.

Fear

Fear is central to adolescence, and it is no different for the boys at Devon. There is a fear of the unknown and a fear of the future, especially during wartime because the future is so unknown. Many of the boys fear going to war for something they do not believe in and other boys, like Finny, fear the seriousness of the situation.

Leper, the only one of the boys who has actually seen war, has a real, deeply ingrained fear, to the point that it makes him crazy and causes him to go AWOL. Seeing what happened to Leper makes the other boys even more fearful of becoming soldiers. Gene is the only one who seems to have fears outside of the war as he obviously fears not being good enough for others and often acts out of jealousy.

Religion

While Devon School gives its students a wholesome, religious education the boys do not necessarily seem religious except for Finny. Finny says his prayers every night and when Gene is with Finny he finds a spiritual beauty in nature and architecture.

After Finny's accident Gene no longer sees beauty in anything and considers his spill into the dirty river with Quackenbush to be a sort of baptism into evil and vengeance. Finny represents God and light in Gene's life as when Finny is not there everything is dark and grim, but when Finny is there Gene sees the light and hope and take the time to pray.

War

War is obviously central to the novel because World War II is going on and the boys are all overcome with thoughts about it and desires to enlist. Devon School begins training the boys for combat, knowing that when they graduate most of the boys will either enlist voluntarily or be drafted.

There are always recruiters coming to the school and Leper actually joins up until he becomes crazy and goes AWOL. Finny does not want to believe in the war and manages to convince himself that it is never really happening until Leper comes back, obviously a changed person. Gene has a sort of internal war going on the entire novel as he feels guilt about what has happened to Finny and a desire to make amends, yet still feels the need to compete with him.

Enmity

Though Gene and Finny are close Gene has made Finny his enemy, though only within his head. Gene has created an envy of Finny that makes him hate his friend, though not knowing how to function without him at the same time; which is ironic because Finny has no hatred in his body and has no use for enemies.

Finny is a genuinely kind and honest person who is not competitive in the least, despite the fact that Gene goes out of his way to compete with Finny, though Finny never seems to notice. Gene tells Finny he would make a bad soldier because he would try to make friends with the enemy and try to play baseball with them because he does not know how to hate or compete. The boys are all expected to hate the opponents in the war though they do not understand why they should hate anyone they do not know.

Chapter Summaries

Chapter One

The novel opens with a grown Gene Forrester (whose
name is not actually revealed until the third chapter)
revisiting Devon School, the boarding school he attended
in his adolescence. He is disappointed that the school has
not changed in fifteen years, as he thought it would have
aged with him. He begins to tour the campus and describes
the buildings in great detail, which seems vibrant despite
the fact that his surroundings are grey and wet as he is in
New Hampshire in November. He finds himself in front of
the school's famed marble staircase which is so hard that it
is not even worn down after all of the years it has been
there. He feels that Devon has changed, though notes that
he still fears some fear at being there. Gene heads to the
tree at the river that changed his life at Devon, noting that
it is bigger and wearier looking than he remembers.

The story flashes back, and Gene is a boy of sixteen
standing by the tree with his friend, Finny. Gene does not
want to climb the tree, despite the fact that Finny insists
that they should. There are three other boys standing by
the tree with them, including Elwin Lepellier ("Leper").

The boys are all deciding whether they are going to climb
the tree and jump off it into the river, which Finny thinks
is a great idea. Finny strips down, and the narrator
comments on his athletic build, and proceeds to climb and
jump out of the tree. Gene feels he must live up to

everyone's expectations and do the same. Once Gene is in the tree he mentally freaks out a bit because he fears that if he does not jump out far enough he will smash his head in the dirt. He begins to resent Finny for getting him into this situation, and then he jumps. None of the other boys would jump, making the bond between Finny and Gene stronger than ever before because they were the only ones brave enough to do it. It is summer session, so there are few students around and no Headmaster. Finny tells Gene he did a good job once he was pressured to jump, as Finny apparently always teases Gene.

The two boys stop and wrestle rather than running when the dinner bell sounds. Realizing they are too late for dinner at this point they return to their dorm and do homework while listening to the radio they smuggled in.

Chapter Two

The next morning a substitute teacher, Mr. Prud'homme, confronts Gene and Finny for missing dinner the night before. Rather than try to make up an excuse for why they missed dinner Finny simply told Mr. Prud'homme the story what happened the night before: the beautiful day, the tree jumping, and the wrestling. The boys manage to get away without being punished, due to Finny's ability to be boisterously friendly and charm the pants off of everyone. When the boys get dressed that day Finny puts on a pink polo shirt in honor of the U.S. having bombed Eastern Europe, though Gene picks on him for looking gay.

That afternoon the boys are set to have tea at the home of their substitute headmaster, Mr. Patch-Withers. It proves an awkward experience for all of the boys and faculty involved, though true to form Finny is the epicenter of lively conversation. In the midst of conversation, Mrs. Patch-Withers sees that Finny is using his school tie as a belt and is horrified. Gene expects that Finny will finally get into trouble, but alas he does not. Finny manages to talk himself out of yet another punishment and at the same time gets the very poker-faced Mr. Patch-Withers to laugh. Gene is at first upset but then congratulates himself for being friends with such a specimen.

As the boys are leaving the party, Finny suggests that they jump out of the tree together this time, as a symbol of solidarity. While they are walking toward the river, Finny states that he does not believe the bombing really happened and Gene agrees, because to the boys at the school the war was just something they heard about rather than something they experienced so to them, it was not real. After the boys swam for a bit, they climbed the tree together to jump in honor of the new society they formed called "The Super Suicide Society of the Summer Session". Gene nearly falls off the branch, and Finny steadies him, then they jump. Gene realizes Finny may have just saved him.

Chapter Three

Gene decides that he does not actually owe Finny any thanks at all because he never would have had a near-death experience had Finny not pressured him to jump from the tree in the first place. Finny decides that other boys must be inducted into their society, and he creates a series of crazy rules, one of which states that Finny and Gene will jump from the tree together at the beginning of every meeting.

The meetings occur every night, and Gene agrees to jump from the tree each time though he always fears he will fall. Finny is an adrenaline junkie only made worse by the fact that the athletic program in the summer is far inferior to the one in the normal school year, and Finny is an athlete. He proceeds to invent a game called "Blitzball" which involves tossing a medicine ball around from boy to boy, with the boy holding the ball becoming a target, and no one ever actually wins the game.

One day when Finny and Gene are at the school swimming pool all by themselves, Finny decides he wants to try to break one of the school records, which he does on the first try. Gene tells Finny to do it again in public, so Gene will not be the only one who has witnessed it, but Finny refuses and tells Gene not to ever tell anyone he did it. Finny decides that the two boys should take a trip to the beach, which is a couple hours by bike and is strictly forbidden by the school.

Gene, of course, agrees, and the boys set out on their trip. Finny greatly enjoys himself at the beach, and, though Gene is not enjoying himself quite as much Finny makes every effort to keep him entertained. They grab a hot dog for dinner and manage to get a couple of beers due to some forged draft cards they were carrying. The boys settle into to sleep on the beach and Finny tells Gene that he is his best friend and he is glad they came to the beach for the day. Gene almost tells Finny that he feels the same but changes his mind at the last minute and says nothing.

Chapter Four

When the boys get back to school in the morning, they are just on time for Gene to take his trigonometry test, which he fails. Gene is very disappointed in failing his test, but Finny distracts him by playing blitzball and having a society meeting. Later that night Finny studies his trigonometry and Finny teases him for trying to be valedictorian. Gene denies his accusations, but when he thinks about it, he realizes that he does want to be valedictorian.

Finny is the star athlete and Gene wants to be the star scholar, to match Finny's athletic accomplishments. In the coming weeks, Gene really buckles down on his studies, and Finny begins to study more as well, Gene believes in an effort to make himself a slightly better student because Gene is a fair athlete and being a fair student rather than a poor one would make Finny equivalent.

Gene senses a faltering in his friendship with Finny because of the obvious jealousy, rivalry, and competition between them but in an attempt to not reveal this feeling to Finny Gene continues attending their society meetings. One night, Finny interrupts Gene's studying to tell him that Leper is going to jump from the tree that night, but Gene believes that Finny only convinced Leper to do it as a means to interrupt Gene's studying. As they head toward the tree Finny, tells Gene he can stay in and study, as he

can tell that Gene is upset. Finny tells Gene that it is good
of him to put so much effort into something he is good at
and that he envies how intelligent and academically
inclined Gene is.

Gene tells Finny that he is done studying, and he wants to
see Leper jump. Gene notes that there must never have
been the rivalry between then that he sensed and that
Finny must definitely be superior to him as it seems
obvious that he is incapable of jealousy. Gene and Finny
climb the tree to jump together, as they do at the start of
every meeting, but Gene's knees buckle, shaking the limb,
and Finny falls to the ground with a heavy thud. Gene
jumps into the water, finally fearless.

Chapter Five

Word spreads around school that Finny's leg is shattered, though no one has been allowed into the infirmary to see him yet. Gene wrestles with the idea that he caused Finny to fall on purpose and wonders if it is true, though he does not seem to know. The only time he feels better about the situation is when he dresses up in one of Finny's outfits, with his pink shirt, but the next morning he is overcome with guilt and anxiety again. Dr. Stanpole tells Gene that Finny is feeling better and would like to see him. He says that Finny's leg is shattered, and he will be able to walk again sometime, but he will never be able to play sports again, a revelation that causes Gene to cry. Dr. Stanhope tells Gene that he must stay strong for Finny.

Gene, still feeling guilty, asks Finny what he remembers about the incident because he wants to know if Finny feels like it is Gene's fault that he fell. Finny hints at the idea that Gene caused the branch to shake on purpose, but immediately recants that notion as he feels terrible for bringing it up at all. When Finny tells Gene that he looked to him for support when he felt he would fall, Gene is outraged, believing that Finny meant to pull him down as well, but Finny says he was merely looking for support.

Gene is about to tell Finny that it is his fault that the branch shook when the doctor comes in and sends Gene away. After that day, Finny is not well enough for visitors and is sent home to Boston as the summer semester ends. When Gene returns to school in September, he stops at Finny's house to see him before continuing his way to Devon. Gene tells Finny that he caused the accident and Finny is outraged and refuses to believe the confession. As Gene is leaving, Finny tells him that he will be back at Devon by late November.

Chapter Six

School has started up again for the fall semester, and Gene
feels like there is something eerie about the campus and
that it is not the same as it was before. The relaxed
teachers and supervisors of the summer are gone, and the
strict teachers are back, disappointed by all of the rule-
breaking they heard occurred over the summer.

At the first church session of the new semester, the leaders
encourage continuity of the standards of Devon, though
Gene feels that they cannot go back to what was before
because everything is different now in the wake of Finny's
accident. He does understand that the rules that are
impressed upon the students are for a reason as Finny got
hurt breaking them.

Gene feels alone in the dorm situation because he is still in
the room he shares with Finny, only Finny has not yet
returned to school, and also Leper has been moved to a
different dorm, so there is a macho alpha male named
Brinker Hadley living across the hall now. Gene is
depressed by this change and feels alone.

School sports have started up again, though Finny is not
there to play them and he will never be able to play again.
Gene heads down to the river for crew practice, though it
is not the river they spent the summer jumping into, it is
the murkier river on campus called the Naguamsett. Gene

arrives at crew late and is harassed by Quackenbush who is a total jerk and hated by everyone.

Gene wants to be crew manager this year, a role usually reserved for someone who is disabled, and is goaded relentlessly for it. He and Quackenbush get into it a bit and end up in the water before Gene is asked to leave. When Gene returns to the dorm, he has a phone call, and it is Finny.

Finny sounds very happy to hear Gene's voice and is happy that his spot as Gene's roommate is still open. In an effort to put aside Gene's "confession" that he caused Finny to fall, he tells Gene that he was awful crazy when he came to visit. Gene agrees with Finny and they begin to talk about sports though Finny is disappointed when he hears Gene wants to be crew manager rather than actually participating. It is obvious that Gene feels he cannot play sports as long as Finny cannot, but Finny tells him that if he cannot play then Gene will play for him.

Chapter Seven

Brinker travels across the hall and into Gene's room, commenting that he is jealous that Gene gets such a large room all to himself. Brinker, seemingly joking, tells Gene he must have pushed Finny out of the tree just so he could live in the big room alone. Gene, feeling quite awkward with his guilt, laughs along with Brinker and suggests they go downstairs to the "Butt Room" in the basement and have a smoke. When the boys arrive downstairs Brinker jokes with the other boys who are down there that he has brought the prisoner, Gene, who has tried to kill his roommate.

Gene keeps joking along with the boys, never denying their accusations. When the boys ask Gene to reenact the scene for them, he feels strange about it and turns attention to a younger boy, who does not realize the other boys are kidding, to do the dirty work. When the boy confirms that he believes Gene must have pushed Finny out of the tree Gene tells the others that he has to go study and leaves the room, never having smoked.

The boys of Devon help to shovel the snow off the train tracks because labor is hard to come by during the war times, and the soldiers need the train tracks clear, so they can travel. Leper does not help the other boys but rather goes off on his cross-country skis to find a beaver dam he heard about. After the tracks are shoveled a train of soldiers rides by and Gene notices that they all look happy and carefree and is jealous of the life experience they are all coming into.

On the way back to Devon, the boys all discuss the idea of leaving school and enlisting though some of them, like Quackenbush, would rather graduate before they join up. Back at Devon the boys see Leper coming back from his trip, and Brinker tells Gene that he is going to leave school, and enlist the next day because he cannot wait any longer. Gene decides that he wants to do the same and will leave the next day as well, but then he returns to his room and finds that Finny has returned.

Chapter Eight

Finny immediately begins picking on Gene, mostly his
clothes which are extremely shabby and filthy after
shoveling the tracks all day. Finny is upset that Devon
does not have maid service this year, but Gene
understands, unselfishly, that with the war going on Devon
is trying to cut back on expenses. The boys go to bed and
Gene prays, which he did not do while Finny was gone.

The next morning Brinker Hadley bursts into the room,
excited about the plans he and Gene have made about
enlisting, but sees Finny and remarks that Gene's plan
must have fallen through, obviously hinting toward the
plan to kill Finny for the room. Gene explains to Finny
that he was considering enlisting, though it is obvious that,
with Finny being back, Gene will not be going anywhere.
Gene feels that Finny needs him around and tells Brinker
that he will not be enlisting with him. After Brinker leaves
Finny and Gene begin to pick on him immediately, and
dub him with the nickname "yellow peril".

When the boys are headed back from chapel, Finny muses
that he loves the winter, and, therefore, the winter must
love him as well because when you love something so
much it has no choice but to love you back. He then
decides that he and Gene should skip class in honor of his
first day back so he can explore the campus. Finny wants
to go to the gym, which is a long trek on crutches and tires

Finny out, but he takes a deep breath and makes a grand entrance into the gym anyway.

Finny wants to visit the locker room first, rather than the trophies, and then asks Gene what sport he is playing. Gene tells Finny that he did not go out for a sport, nor did he decide to manage the crew team, he is just going to gym class. Finny is flabbergasted and insists that Gene allow Finny to train him for the 1944 Olympics, as that is what Finny was going to do before he got hurt.

Gene tells Finny that, with the war, there will be no Olympics, but Finny sticks to his story that there is no war and a bunch of fat old men made it up to keep the country in line and tells Gene the reason he is privy to this information is because of the amount of suffering he has been through, a sentiment, which both boys seem shocked was mentioned. Gene proceeds to do chin-ups, thirty of them at the urging of Finny.

One day when Gene is running he feels different than ever before like he finally hit his stride and Finny is impressed. When Mr. Ludsbury asks what they were doing Finny tells him that they are training for the Olympics and when Mr. Ludsbury tells him that all training must be for war purposes, Finny simply says to him, "no". Finny tells Gene that Mr. Ludsbury is too thin to be in on the fat old man plot.

Chapter Nine

Gene decides that he will go along with Finny's view that there is no war going on, not because he believes it but because it makes life more carefree and enjoyable. Leper enlisted in the service which came as a big surprise to everyone because he is the last person they expected to enlist. Some recruiters came to Devon one day and showed the boys videos of the soldiers skiing, which sparked Leper's interest and he decided that if he can ski as a soldier then he wants to enlist immediately. He enlisted just before he turned eighteen, so he was able to choose what he wanted to do, rather than be drafted and forced into something.

Gene thought that if Brinker had gone in first then it would awaken the boys to the reality of the war, and they could stop pretending it was happening, but Leper was not a significant enough member of the Devon community to have that kind of effect on the student body. From that point on whenever the boys heard about something big happening in the war, like an attempt to kill Hitler, they assumed that Leper must have been the one to do it, which made the war stories much more fun and interesting to discuss. Finny was the only one who did not subscribe to this mindset and instead immersed himself in training Gene for the Olympics, which was an attempt to keep Gene away from the war talk, as well.

Gene notes that Saturdays at Devon are extremely boring, and the boys must invent numerous activities to entertain themselves. One day Finny brings up the idea of having a carnival the following weekend and Gene agrees. The boys come up with prizes to give away for the winners of the events and Brinker even goes along with the idea and has fun with it, despite his recent role as a serious student.

The boys drink some hard cider, start to have a good time and Finny signifies the beginning of the games by burning a copy of "The Iliad". Finny gets Gene to show off his Olympic skills and soon after Gene gets a telegram. The telegram is from Leper who has "escaped" and is hiding "at the Christmas location," and he wants Gene to come to him right away. Leper signs the note "your best friend".

Chapter Ten

Gene leaves that night to go to Leper's house in Vermont, as it is obviously the Christmas location he not-so-cryptically mentioned in the telegram. Gene, as the narrator, muses that he would make the same journey many times in his life when he is in the military, though, he never actually saw combat because the war was basically over by the time he enlisted. Gene tells himself that Leper has just escaped from some spies because there is no way that he escaped the army.

Leper seems happy to see Gene, but he is acting strange. Leper seems extremely jumpy and emotional, and Gene asks him how long he is on leave before he has to go back. Leper tells Gene that he went AWOL (absent without leave) before they could dismiss him for being mentally insane, formally called a "section eight". Gene is scared of Leper at this point because he is very different from the friend that left Devon. Gene lashes out at Leper out of fear and Leper throws Finny's accident in his face, accusing Gene of pushing Finny out of the tree.

Gene attacks Leper which attracts the attention of Mrs. Lepellier. Gene tries to explain himself to Leper's mother and apologizes to her and stays for lunch at Leper's request because he felt bad if he refused the offer. After lunch, the boys go for a walk and Gene feels like being in nature will bring out the old Leper, though he is mistaken.

Leper tells Gene about all of the crazy images and dreams he would have in the army--about things transforming into other things. Gene feels really odd and uncomfortable around Leper at this point and starts yelling at Leper to stop telling him these things as they have nothing to do with him. He runs away from Leper's house right back towards the town and Devon.

Chapter Eleven

When Gene gets back to campus he wants to see Finny because Finny's mind is always on sports, rather than war. Ironically, Finny is involved in a snowball fight with some other boys when Gene returns. Gene is distracted by the way Finny walks; he used to almost float and now he seems so crippled, aside from the fact that his leg is in a cast.

Finny asks about Leper and Gene keeps the gory details to himself. Gene tells Finny that he should be more careful and perhaps not do things like get into snowball fights because he may break his leg again, but Finny tells him that he thinks that once a bone grows back together it is stronger than it was to begin with. Later Brinker comes into Finny and Gene's room and asks about Leper. Gene tells the other two boys that Leper went AWOL, and Brinker assumes correctly that Leper went crazy. Finny finally begins to admit that the war must be real because fake wars do not make people crazy.

Devon becomes immersed in the war and everything to do with it while Brinker, one of the boys who most wanted to enlist, finds himself interested in anything that has nothing to do with the war. Brinker tells Gene that the reason he did not enlist is because of Finny and Gene does not confirm or deny this accusation. Brinker brings up the old "joke" that Gene pushed Funny off the tree, and Gene gets a little uneasy over the whole situation.

One night while the boys are studying Finny says that he saw Leper on campus, and Gene remembers that Leper thinks he pushed Finny out of the tree, so Gene gets very uncomfortable at the thought of him being back at Devon. Later that night Brinker invites Finny and Gene to come out with him and his friends as he has a set of keys to the whole campus from being involved in so many clubs. The boys sneak out and end up in the Assembly Room where Brinker immediately begins making fun of Finny's limp.

Brinker begins asking Finny what happened on the day Finny fell, determined to get to the bottom of the whole situation, much to Gene's horror. Finny's story changes numerous times as it becomes clear that he does not entirely remember what happened that day, he even thinks the tree may have shaken itself on purpose. Brinker and his friends decide they need to bring in a witness and get Leper. Leper refuses to answer any questions about the incident as he does not want to implicate himself and says a few other crazy things.

Finny gets angry at the spectacle, tells all the boys he does not care what happened that day and storms from the room. After Finny leaves the room the boys hear him fall the very large, very hard, marble staircase.

Chapter Twelve

Gene remembers every acting very responsible and exactly as they should in the wake of Finny's accident. They held him still while someone went to fetch Dr. Stanpole and the wrestling coach, Phil Latham. Gene finds it strange to watch Finny being carried out because the only person Finny has ever needed help from was Gene, in any other case Finny was the one doing the helping. Dr. Stanpole says that Finny's leg is, in fact, broken again, but this time it is not shattered it is a clean break and should heal just fine after surgery.

All of the boys are told to go back to their rooms, but Gene finds himself crouching in the bushes in the dark outside of the infirmary rather than going to his room. He hears the conversation between Finny and the doctors and begins making jokes with himself while he waits. Eventually once Finny is alone Gene calls out his name and crawls through the window.

Finny begins yelling at Gene, asking him if there is another bone in his body he would like to break while Gene apologizes fruitlessly. Gene leaves the infirmary but rather than go back to his dorm he wanders around campus, finding himself outside of the gym which looks strange to him. Gene feels as though he no longer exists, or maybe he never did; perhaps he was nothing more than a ghost all his years at Devon. Gene falls asleep leaning against the wall of the stadium.

The next morning Gene returns to the dorm and finds a note for him from Dr. Stanpole asking him to bring some of Finny's clothes down to the infirmary. Gene grabs some of Finny's clothes and sets out for the infirmary, feeling as though he is experiencing déjà vu, which, in a way, he is as this happened just last summer. He gets to the room and finds Finny alone and tries to explain himself. Gene apologizes, just as he did in Boston, and Finny tells him that the whole situation would be different if there were no war because Finny feels helpless having a broken leg and not being able to fight.

Gene tells Finny that he would be no good in a war anyway because he is too friendly and would probably try to make friends with the enemy. Gene and Finny agree that the tree situation was an accident, and not intentional at all and Finny goes in for surgery. When Gene returns to see Finny after his surgery he is greeted by Dr. Stanpole who tells him that Finny died during his surgery. It seems that a piece of marrow broke off and floated up to his heart, killing him. Gene tells the reader that he never once cried about Finny, not even at his funeral, because it would be like crying at his own funeral as Finny was a part of him.

Chapter Thirteen

As school was coming to a close that spring, some jeeps filled with troops rolled into the far common. Brinker and Gene went out to the common to see the greeting ceremony that is happening, and Brinker brings up Leper, but Gene does not want to talk about him, or about Finny. Gene feels as though peace no longer exists for anyone, even at Devon, except maybe for the boys who were there during the summer session.

Brinker introduces Gene to his father who reminds Gene of one of the fat old men who made up the story of the war happening that Finny always used to talk about. Mr. Hadley likes to talk about war and the boys' responsibility to fight, which Brinker apologizes to Gene for but Gene thinks he knows where Mr. Hadley is coming from. He thinks that Brinker and Finny were similar in the way that they tried to rebel to forget that the war was happening at all.

Gene does not believe that war is the fault of the fat old men, but of ignorance in the hearts of many men. While Gene is clearing out his gym locker he thinks about Finny as he often does though he refuses to talk about him with anyone because Finny is not dead to him. Finny's way of living still resides in Gene, even as he is telling the story. Finny never had any hatred for anyone or any enemies as most people did.

Gene says that most people find something to hate and spend their whole life making that one thing their eternal enemy, though Finny never did that. Gene says that he went to war though he killed no one and never hated any of his opponents because he knew Finny would not have. Gene says that the only enemy he ever had he killed while he was at Devon.

About BookCaps

We all need refreshers every now and then. Whether you are a student trying to cram for that big final, or someone just trying to understand a book more, BookCaps can help. We are a small, but growing company, and are adding titles every month.

Visit www.bookcaps.com to see more of our books, or contact us with any questions.